Mel Bay Presents

&Trem &Octave
Harmonica Method

by Phil Duncan

To access the online audio go to:
www.melbay.com/96317BCDEB

Cover photo courtesy of Hohner Harmonicas

MW00861826

Online Audio Tracks

Visit us on the Web at www.melbay.com — E-mail us at email@melbay.com

Table of Contents

About this Book

There are several different models of 40 reed, 20 hole double reed tremolo harmonicas. Basically, one begins with hole one C (do) and the others begins with hole 2 E (mi).

This book will concentrate on 40 reed, 20 hole double reed tremolo or octave harmonica in C, hole one is C (do). Because the hole one C (do) double reed harmonica is most like the diatonic 10 hole standard harmonica.

However, most double reed harmonicas, including the octave tuned harmonicas, can be used with this book. This book will examine the differences between each instrument and application.

Take Care of Your Harmonica

Do not blow or draw too hard, it unnecessarily strains the reeds. Control saliva. Teach yourself to play with a fairly dry mouth. Keeping your head up always helps. Always tap the harmonica mouth piece on the "palm" of the hand to remove any excess saliva or foreign substances. Do not play while chewing gum or eating candy.

How to Hold Your Double-Reed Harmonica

Hold the harmonica firmly in the left hand with hole number one or the lowest pitch to the left. The left index and middle fingers should lie along the upper part of the instrument and the thumb along the lower part.

The double reed harmonica that is longer than 16 holes cannot usually be held in the V of the hand. Like the chromatic harmonica, it must stick out past the V of the hand. The right hand should be cupped around the back side of harmonica. The heel of both hands should stay in contact.

Vibrato

By opening and closing the right hand on the backside of the instrument can creat a vibrato that will intensify the tremolo effect. Using breath control, puffing air, sometimes called the diapharam vibrato, can also increase the tremolo effect.

Double-Reed Tremolo Harmonica

On some harmonicas numbers are not imprinted on the cover. You may want to etch numbers on your harmonica for quick reference. Etch numbers over every two horizontal holes.

If your harmonica starts with C (do) in the first hole on the left, then number the first two holes "1". See example 1.

If your harmonica starts with E (mi) in the first hole on the left, then number the first two holes "2". See example 2.

That way hole 4 is always "C" (do) blow and "d" (re) draw. Some 40 reed 20 hole tremolos start on C (do) and some 40 reed 20 hole tremolos start with E (mi).

Example 1
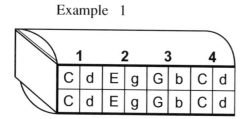

Example 2
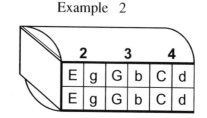

The tremolo harmonica produces sound by using two reeds instead of one. *There is never a blow reed and a draw reed in the same vertical pair of holes.* The tremolo effect is produced by a very slight difference in tuning each pair of reeds. In other words each reed is slightly out of pitch with its pair.

The two pitches then vibrate creating an "accordion" or "chorus" sound. In addition to a complete scale, it has portions suited to playing arpeggios and chords.

Tremolo

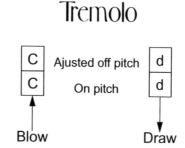

Generally, the double reed tremolo or octave harmonica is played like the 10 hole standard diatonic harmonica. Which is why most veteran players recommend that you learn the 10 hole diatonica harmonica first, then progress to the double reed instruments.

"Single" Tone

In this book the "UPPER CASE" alphabet letters are blow tones and the "lower case" letters are draw.

Producing a single tone will seem easier to play on the double reed harmonica. That's because you don't have to be quite as careful with the placement of the lips to play a "single" tone. You actually expose **two** double holes, **two** for blow and **two** for draw. Therefore, the area is larger. This gives you more room to play the "single" note. Tongue blocking, either on the left or the right, is the traditional technique for playing a single tone.

Tongue Blocking to the Left

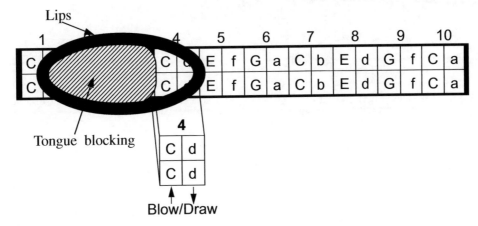

Tongue Blocking to the Right

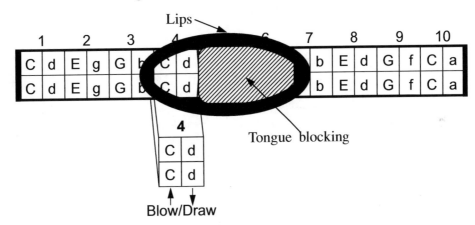

Tongue Blocking in the Middle (Octaves on the Tremolo)

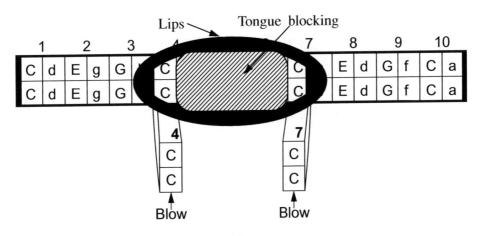

Lip Blocking Technique

It is possible to play single tones using the lip blocking technique, that is, pursing the lips like to whistle. *Most beginners and many veteran players use this technique because it appears to be easier.* However, it is recommended that traditional tongue blocking should also be learned.

Lip Blocking

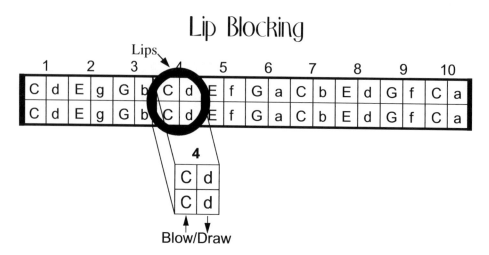

The 40 reed, 20 hole tremolo or harmonica in C (C - do first hole) is suitable for most playing purposes. This tremolo or octave harmonica is an excellent solo instrument. It is much like the 10 hole standard harmonica.

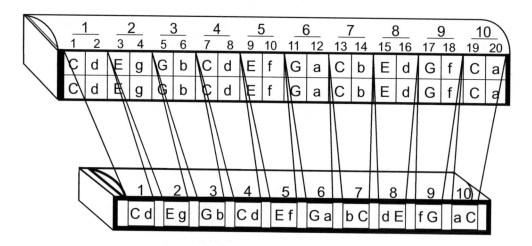

The first set of tones, holes 1 through 6, are just like the 10 hole standard harmonica. And just like the 10 hole standard harmonica you begin playing in hole 4. Howerver, to finish the scale notice on the tremolo that 7 draw is to the right of blow 7.

At first, this change is not noticed because the mouth opening moves to hole 7 with both blow and draw. However, by not moving far enough over, draw 7 may not play.

The above illustration also shows holes 7 through 10 reversed on the tremolo. If you lip block all four cells, blow and draw, as you move up the scale on the tremolo, you will not notice any difference except in the distance you need to move over to get the quad holes positioned for playing. This greater distance will take additional practice to master.

Double-Reed <u>Octave</u> Tuned Harmonica

The double reed octave tuned hormonica is designed the same as the tremolo harmonica except the top row of tones are an octave lower than the bottom row.

The resulting sound is stronger and more full bodied, but without the tremolo effect. It may be necessary to have at least a 40 reed 20 hole octave tuned double reed instrument to play all of the music in this book.

Octave Tuned

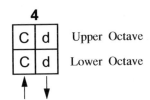

Huang Double-Reed Tremolo Harmonicas

The exception to all of this is the Musettes (tremolo harmonicas) and Cathedral Concert (octave tuned) designed by Cham Ber Huang. His tremolo and octave harmonicas play exactly like a 12 hole solo tuned harmonica. That is, there are double C's at each inner octave. It is a 24 hole double reed, diatonic, solo tuned instrument.

If you play chromatic harmonica, this is natural. There are no changes. Even the amount of movement is the same on the chromatic harmonica as the "Huang Musettes" tremolo and "Cathedral Concert" octave harmonicas.

These harmonicas come in a case of two tremolo's or they can be purchased separately. One is in the key of C and the other is in the key of C sharp. Using them both, stacked, you can also play "chromatically". Using the Huang double reed instruments in C and C♯; you can play any music that requires a chromatic harmonica. The numbering (which is not stamped on these harmonicas) is the same displacement as the 12 hole harmonica.

Huang's 3 Octave Tremolo (Musette) &
Octave-Tuned (Cathedral Concert) Harmonicas

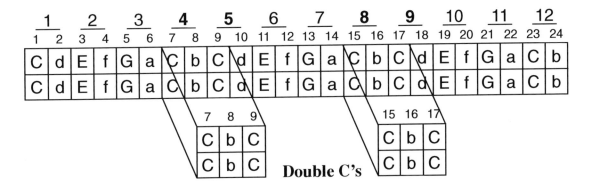

For more tunes to play on the Tremolo and Octave Harmonicas see: *Stephen Fosters Songs for Harmonica* and *Irish Tunes for Harmonica* by Phil Duncan, available from Mel Bay Publications, Inc.

A whole note recieves 4 counts.	$\mathbf{o}$ = 4
A half note recieves 2 count.	$\d$ = 2
A quartet note recieves 1 count.	$\quarternote$ = 1

Lip Blocking

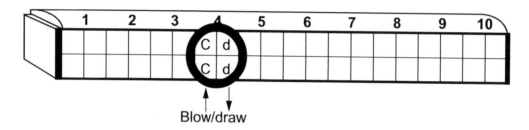

Blow/draw

C

"C" is on the leger line below the staff.
It is a blow note in the 4th hole.

Hole 4 Blow, the "C" Note

1.

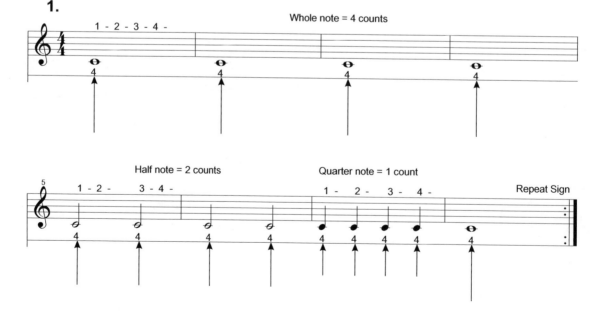

d

"**d**" is on the space below the staff.
It is a draw note in the 4th hole.

Hole 4 Blow and Draw, "C" and "d"

2.

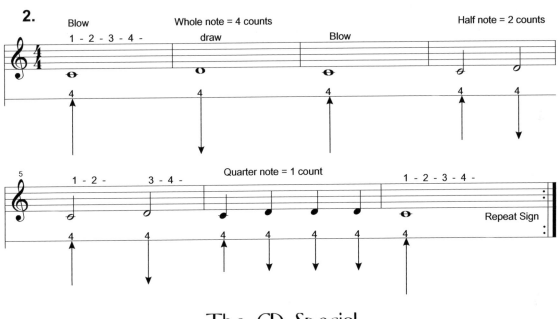

The CD Special

3.

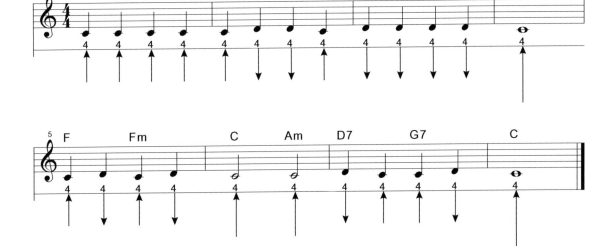

Lip Blocking

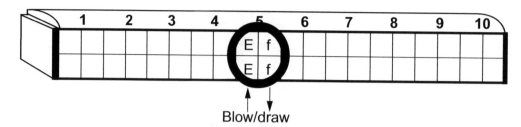

E

"**E**" is on the bottom line of the staff.
It is a blow note in the 5th hole.

The **quartet rest** is one count of silence.
No air through the harmonica.

Easy "E"

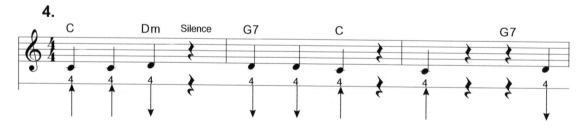

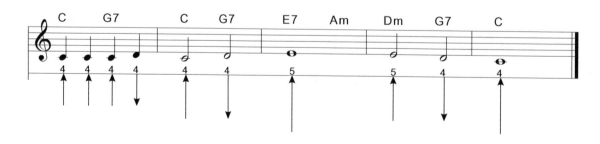

Take it EZ

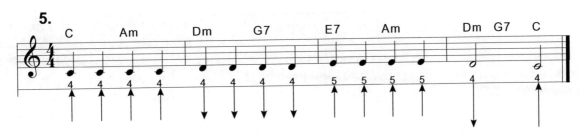

Hot Cross Buns

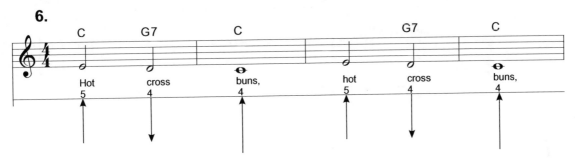

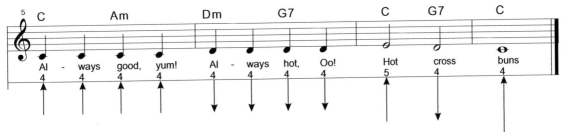

Merrily We Roll Along

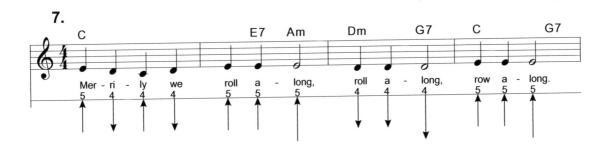

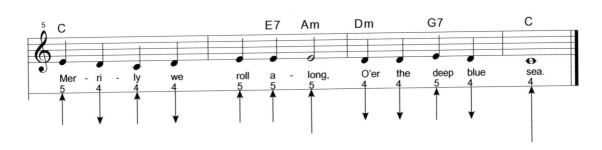

Tongue Blocking

Using tongue blocking can enhance your playing. It is simply done by placing the tongue on the holes to the left of the tone you want to play, then blow or draw air on the right inside of the mouth. To produce a chord you lift your tongue and quickly reset it back on the harmonica mouth piece blocking the same holes again. This will create a single tone, then a chord, and then a single tone. Your tongue can do this rhythmically, that is tapping a rhythm on the mouth piece while blowing or drawing air. The single tone plays all the time, tongue on or off.

Single Tone, Blow or Draw – Tongue ON

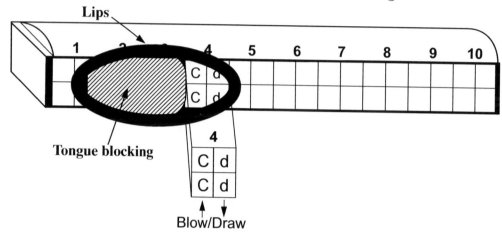

Single Tone with Chord, Blow or Draw – Tongue Off

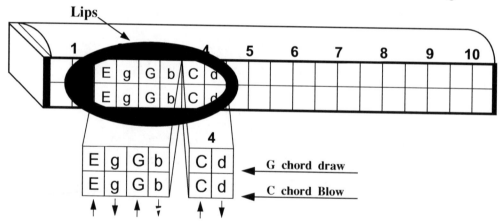

NOTICE: The curved ⌒ line is a tie.
This lengthens the sound of the first note through the 2nd note or additional same notes. See Number 16.

8. Tongue:

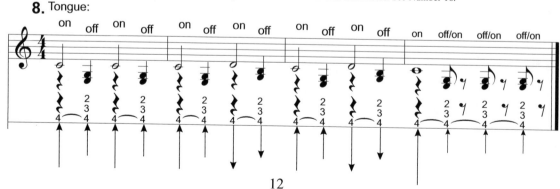

Single Tone, Blow or Draw – Tongue ON

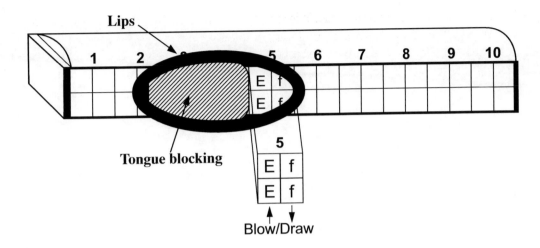

Single Tone with Chord, Blow or Draw – Tongue Off

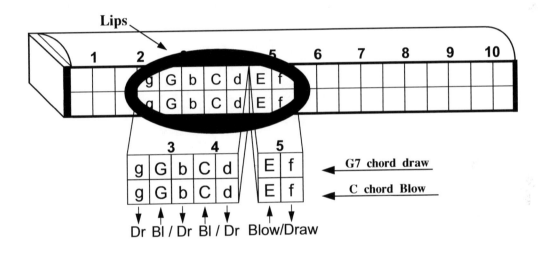

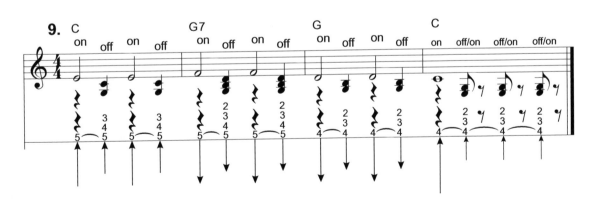

Hot Cross Buns
Tongue Blocking

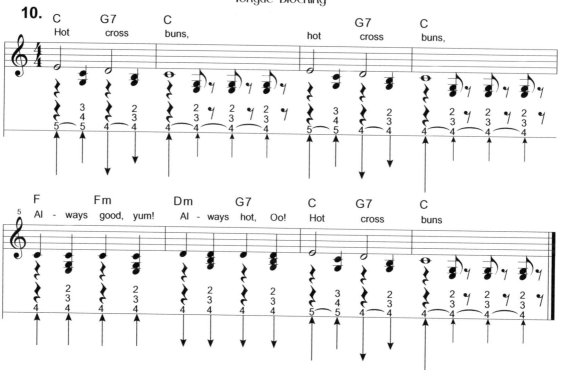

Merrily We Roll Along
Tongue Blocking

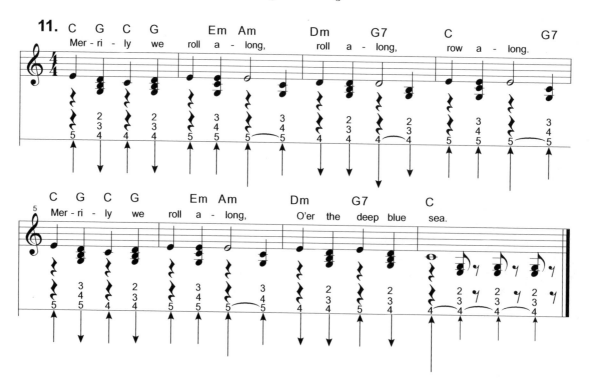

Tongue blocking is the same for each set of holes. Continue to develop the tongue blocking method on each example and song, along with the lip blocking trchnique.

You can also tongue block on the right side of the single tone. The air would come down the left inside of the mouth. The same chords will sound with a higher pitch than the single tone.

f

"**f**" is on the bottom space of the staff.
It is a draw tone on the 5th hole.

Hole 5, Draw "f"

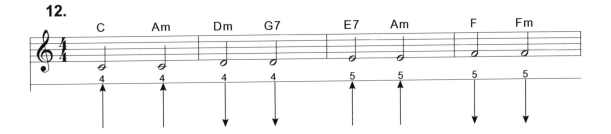

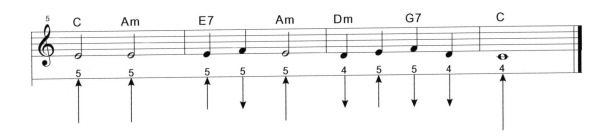

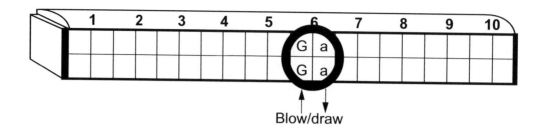

Blow/draw

G

"**G**" is on the 2nd line of the staff.
It is a Blow tone in the 6th hole.

A dotted half note ♩· = 3 counts.

The dotted half note is worth 3 quarter notes.
The dot gets one half of the
value of the note.

5 Tone Scale

13.

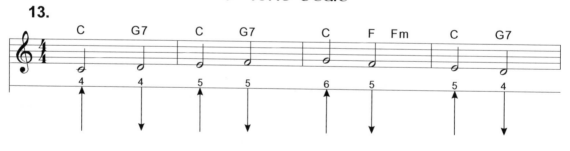

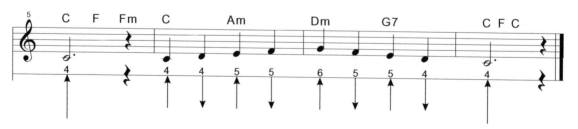

Some Folks Do

S. Foster

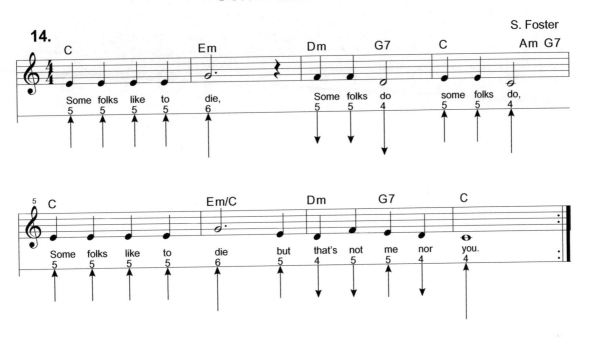

14.

| C | Em | Dm | G7 | C | Am G7 |

Some folks like to die, / Some folks do / some folks do,
5 5 5 5 6 / 5 5 4 / 5 5 4

5 | C | Em/C | Dm | G7 | C |

Some folks like to die / but that's not me nor you.
5 5 5 5 6 / 5 4 5 5 4 4

First and second endings were created to shorten the printing of music.
Play the music the first time then repeat. Do not play the 1st ending again,
skip the 1st ending and play the 2nd ending.

I Know Where I'm Going

15.

Ballad

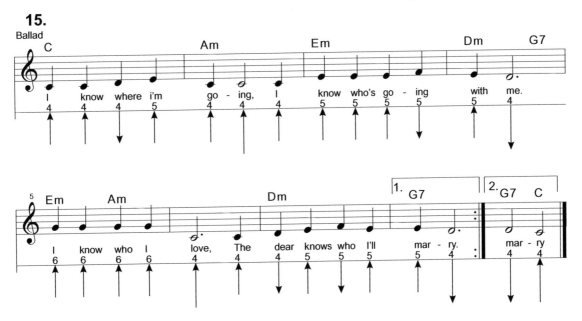

| C | Am | Em | Dm | G7 |

I know where i'm go - ing, I know who's go - ing with me.
4 4 4 5 4 4 4 5 5 5 5 5 4

5 | Em | Am | Dm | 1. G7 | 2. G7 C |

I know who I love, The dear knows who I'll mar - ry. / mar - ry
6 6 6 6 4 4 4 5 5 5 5 4 / 4 4

17

TIE notes are two or more notes of the same pitch, connected by a curved line, that increase the length of sound. The first tie note is sounded and second is held. <u>Do not</u> resound the second note, only hold it out for the total value of both notes.

Pick-up notes are notes at the beginning that do not start on count one. The other count(s) are usually found at the end of the song.

Oh, When the Saints

16.

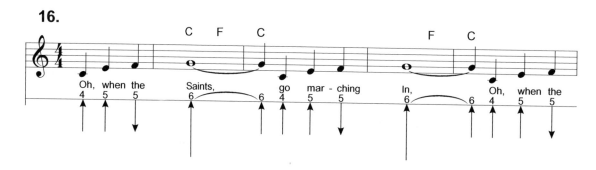

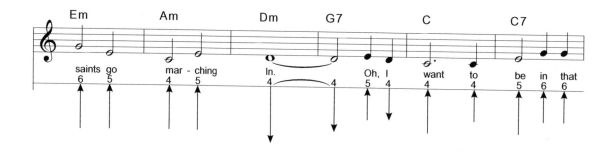

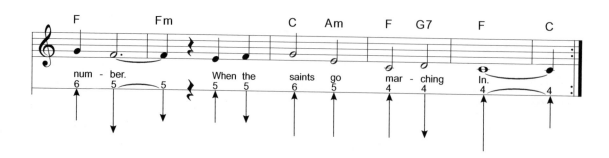

Ode to Joy

L. Beethoven

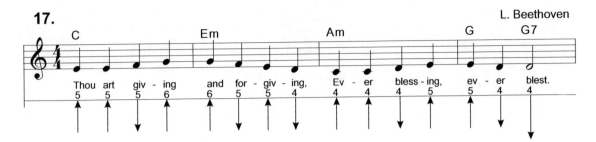

Thou art giv - ing and for - giv - ing, Ev - er bless - ing, ev - er blest.

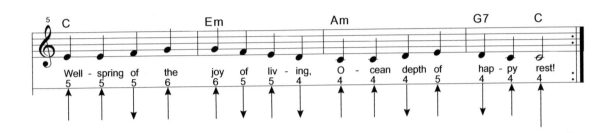

Well - spring of the joy of liv - ing, O - cean depth of hap - py rest!

Slurs are two "different" notes connected by a curved line to be played very smoothly. **Slurs** are not to be confused with tie notes of the "same" pitch.

Jingle Bells

18.

Pierpoint

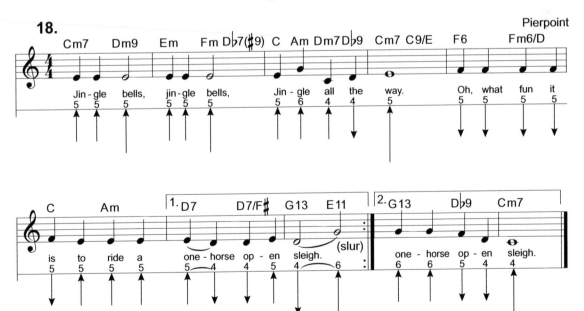

Jin - gle bells, jin - gle bells, Jin - gle all the way. Oh, what fun it

is to ride a one - horse op - en sleigh. (slur) one - horse op - en sleigh.

a

"a" is on the 2nd space of the staff.
It is a draw tone on the 6th hole.

Time Signature

The top number tells the number of counts per measure.
The bottom number tells the kind of note that equals one count.

4 = counts per measure

4 = kind of note that is worth one count (quarter note)

Waltz time: 3 counts per measure.

Beautiful Brown Eyes

19.

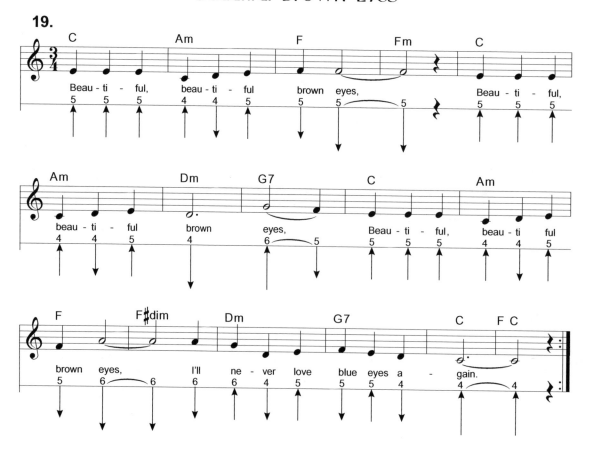

"Fine" means the end of the song.
"C" is on the left of "b", but the draw tone is lower

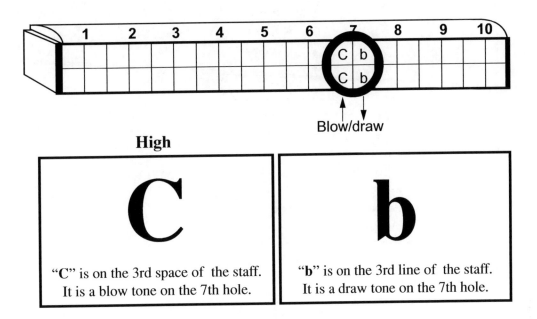

High

C

"**C**" is on the 3rd space of the staff.
It is a blow tone on the 7th hole.

b

"**b**" is on the 3rd line of the staff.
It is a draw tone on the 7th hole.

The Marines' Hymn

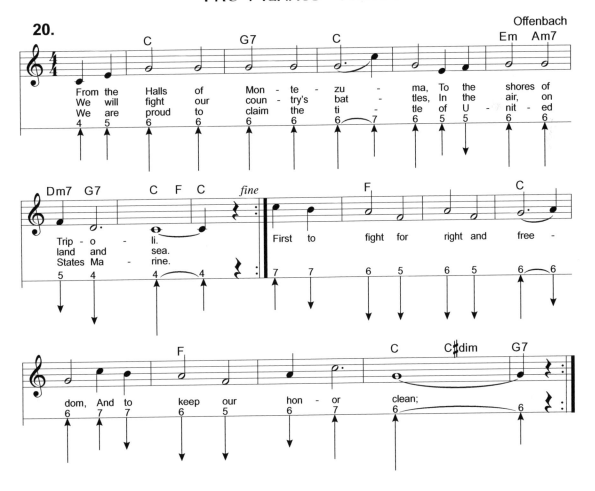

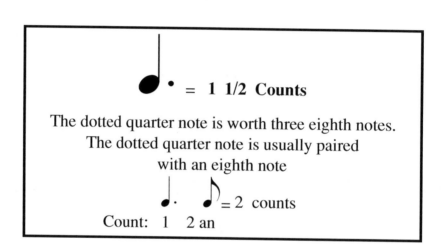

EIGHTH NOTE

= 1/2 count

It takes **two** eighth notes
to equal **one** quarter note

♪♪ = ♩

Multiple eighth notes are barred together.

If tapping the foot, the half count is when the toe is up.

♩· = 1 1/2 Counts

The dotted quarter note is worth three eighth notes.
The dotted quarter note is usually paired
with an eighth note

♩· ♪ = 2 counts

Count: 1   2 an

Peg Leg

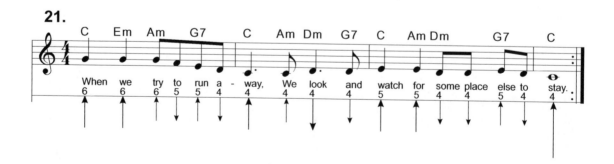

21.

| C | Em | Am | G7 | C | Am Dm | G7 | C | Am Dm | G7 | C |

When we   try to run a - way,   We look and watch for some place else to stay.
6   6   6   5   5   4   4   4   4   4   5   5   4   4   5   4   4

She Wore a Yellow Ribbon

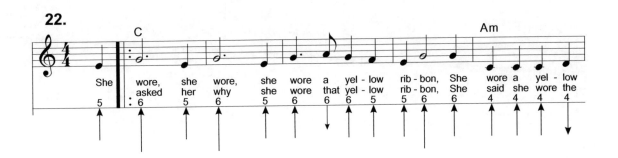

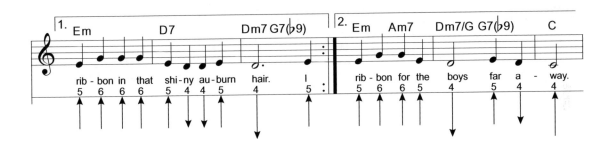

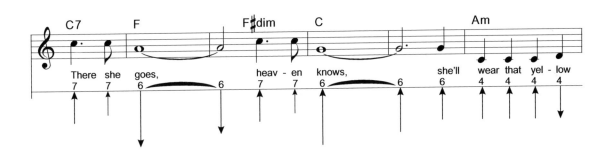

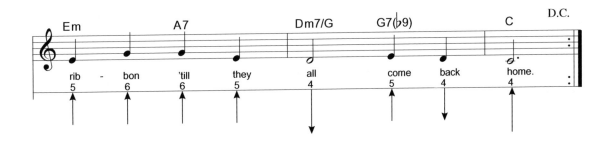

Wearing of the Green

23.

Believe Me, If All Those Endearing Young Charms
Thomas Moore

24.

"E" is on the left of "d", the draw tone is lower

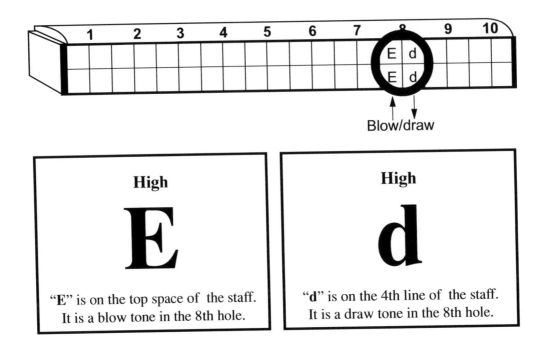

Blow/draw

<table>
<tr><td>

High

E

"E" is on the top space of the staff.
It is a blow tone in the 8th hole.

</td><td>

High

d

"d" is on the 4th line of the staff.
It is a draw tone in the 8th hole.

</td></tr>
</table>

D. S. al fine: Means to go back to the sign (𝄋) and repeat to *"fine"*.

Old Folks at Home
Swanee River

S.C. Foster

An eighth rest (𝄾) is worth 1/2 count of silence.

Little Brown Jug

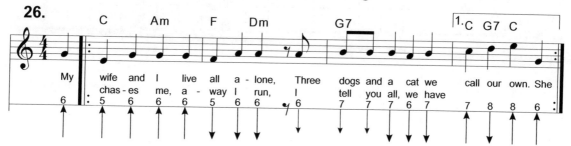

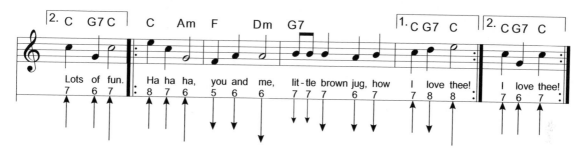

Wildwood Flower

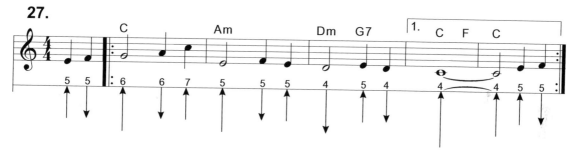

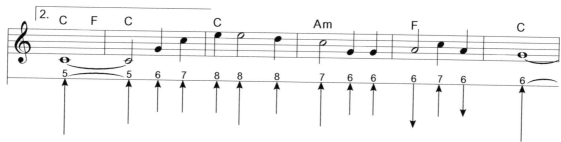

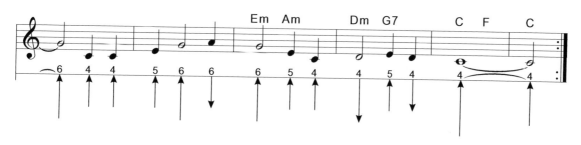

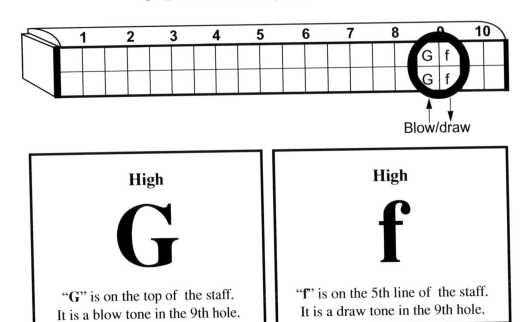

Blow/draw

High **G**	High **f**
"G" is on the top of the staff. It is a blow tone in the 9th hole.	"f" is on the 5th line of the staff. It is a draw tone in the 9th hole.

The Yellow Rose of Texas

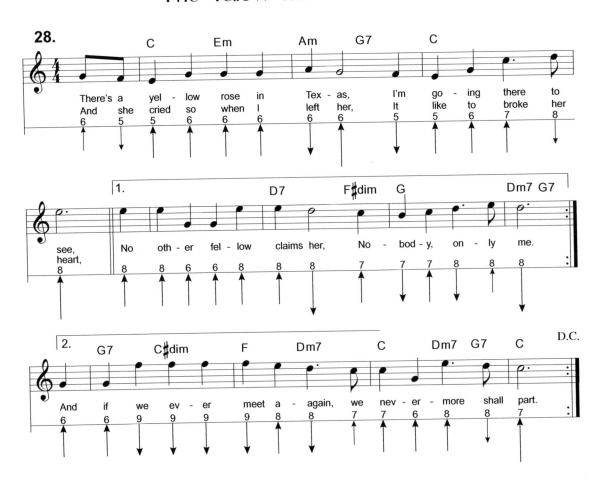

28

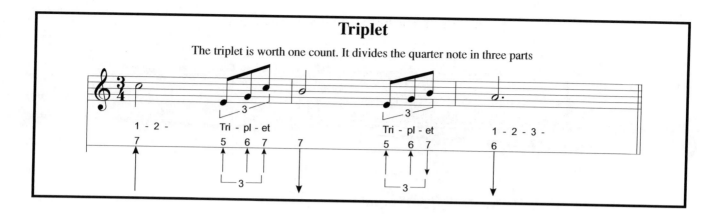

Triplet

The triplet is worth one count. It divides the quarter note in three parts

La Boheme

29.

G. Puccini

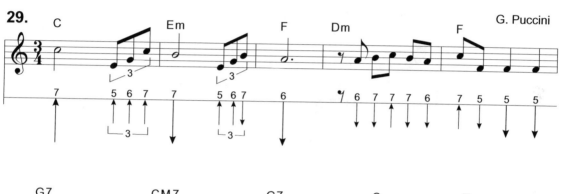

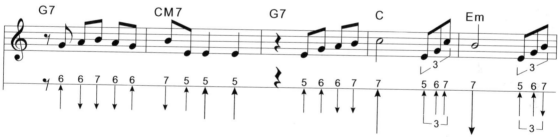

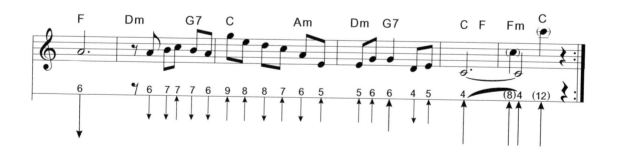

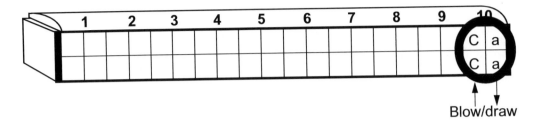

Blow/draw

There is no "b" tone on the harmonica that begins with "C" in the first hole.

Double High # C "C" is on the 2nd leger line above the staff. It is a blow tone in the 10th hole.	**High** # a "a" is on the 1st leger line above the staff. It is a draw tone in the 10th hole.

Grace Notes
Musical Ornamentation

It is played in time with the note that follows.

Embellishment by the performer

Cut time also known as "Alle Breve" which is half of common time. Instead of 4 counts per measure it is 2 counts per measure. The half note gets 1 count. There are several ways this is shown.

C is for common time or 4/4 time. is for cut time or 2/2 time.

Turkey in the Straw

Lip Blocking

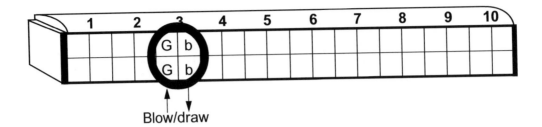

Blow/draw

<table>
<tr><td align="center">Low

G</td><td align="center">Low

b</td></tr>
<tr><td align="center">"G" is below the 2nd leger line
below the staff.
It is a blow tone on the 3rd hole.</td><td align="center">"b" is below the 1st leger line
below the staff.
It is a draw tone on the 3rd hole.</td></tr>
</table>

Down in the Valley

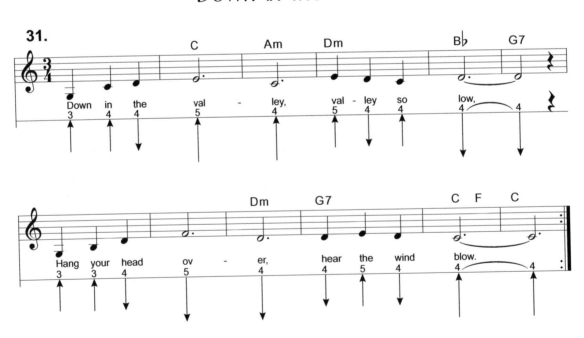

31.

Down in the val - ley, val - ley so low,
3   4   4   5   4   5   4   4   4   4

Hang your head ov - er, hear the wind blow.
3   3   4   5   4   4   5   4   4   4

The Irish hornpipe is played with a swing on eighth notes. The dotted eighth and sixteenth notes represent this beat pattern. (♪. ♪)

32

The Galway Hornpipe

*⑥ Bend Hole "6" down 1/2 step

Sweet Molly Malone
Cockles and Mussels

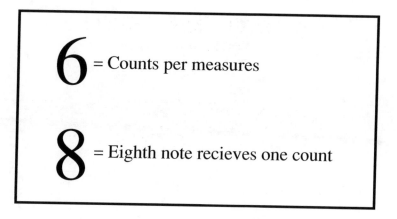

Time Signature Values

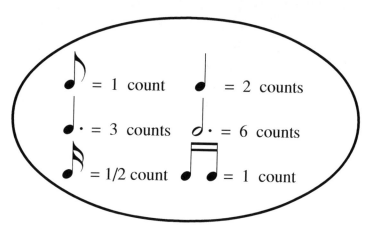

The Worms Crawl

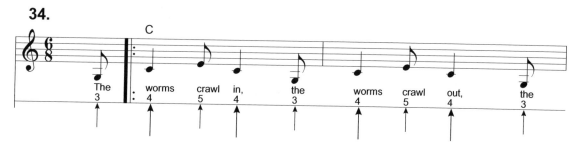

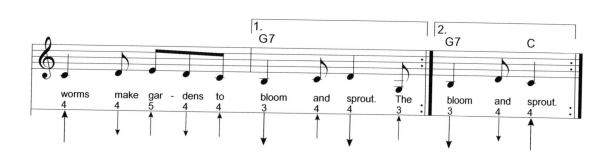

The House of the Rising Sun

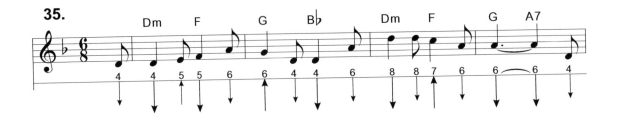

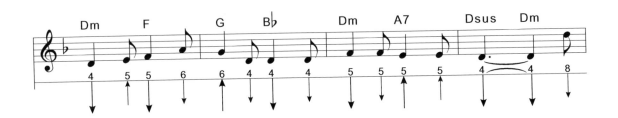

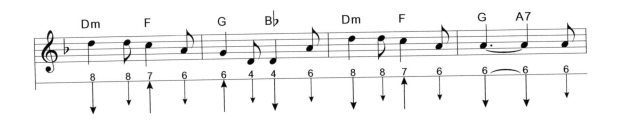

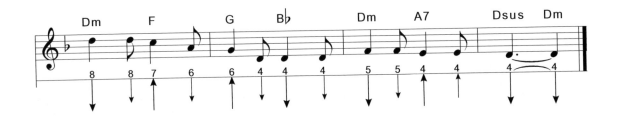

The Irish Washerwoman

36.

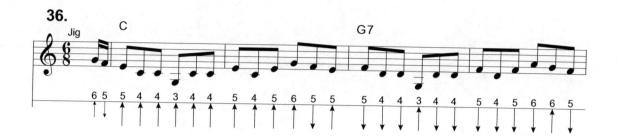

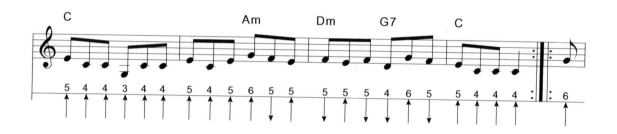

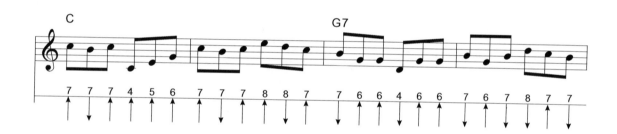

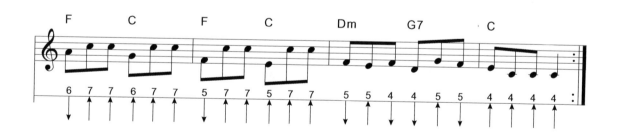

Here We Come A-Caroling

Lower Octave

F and A are missing : This is designed for chords

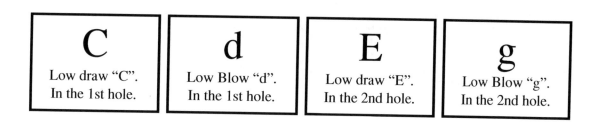

	C										
	C	d	E	g							
	C	d	E	g							

C	d	E	g
Low draw "C". In the 1st hole.	Low Blow "d". In the 1st hole.	Low draw "E". In the 2nd hole.	Low Blow "g". In the 2nd hole.

There tones, holes 1 and 2, usually form chords on the lower end
of the harmonica for use with tongue blocking.

Holes 1, 2 and 3 blow from the C chord (C-E-G) on the C harmonica.
Holes 1, 2 and 3 draw from the G chord (G-B-D).

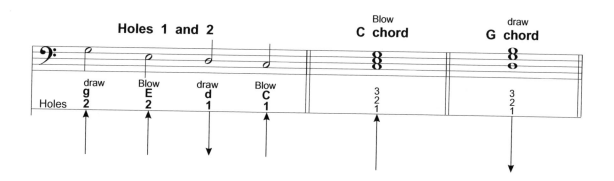

Double-Reed Harmonica Models

On double sided octave tuned and tremolos, one side will begin with "Do",
the other side will begin with "Mi".
The double sided harmonica comes in two keys,
such as C-G, A-D, B flat-F.

14 Hole Harmonica (Mi)

| Complete Scale |

2	3	4	5	6	7	8

| E | g | G | b | C | d | E | f | G | a | C | b | E | d |
| E | g | G | b | C | d | E | f | G | a | C | b | E | d |

This harmonica starts on hole 2 "E" (Mi)

****

16 Hole Harmonica (Mi)

| Complete Scale |

2	3	4	5	6	7	8	9

| E | g | G | b | C | d | E | f | G | a | C | b | E | d | G | f |
| E | g | G | b | C | d | E | f | G | a | C | b | E | d | G | f |

This harmonica starts on hole 2 "E" (Mi)

****

20 Hole Harmonica (Mi)

| Complete Scale |

2	3	4	5	6	7	8	9	10	11

| E | g | G | b | C | d | E | f | G | a | C | b | E | d | G | f | C | a | E | b |
| E | g | G | b | C | d | E | f | G | a | C | b | E | d | G | f | C | a | E | b |

This harmonica starts on hole 2 "E" (Mi)

****

20 Hole Harmonica (Do)

| Complete Scale |

1	2	3	4	5	6	7	8	9	10

| C | d | E | g | G | b | C | d | E | f | G | a | C | b | E | d | G | f | C | a |
| C | d | E | g | G | b | C | d | E | f | G | a | C | b | E | d | G | f | C | a |

This harmonica starts on hole 1 "C" (do)

40

24 Hole Harmonica (Mi)

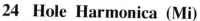

Complete Scale

2		3		4		5		6		7		8		9		10		11		12		13	
E	g	G	b	C	d	E	f	G	a	C	b	E	d	G	f	C	a	E	b	G	d	C	f
E	g	G	b	C	d	E	f	G	a	C	b	E	d	G	f	C	a	E	b	G	d	C	f

This harmonica starts on hole 2 "E" (Mi)

****

30 Hole Harmonica (Do)

Complete Scale

1		2		3		4		5		6		7		8		9		10		11		12		13		14		15	
C	d	E	g	G	b	C	d	E	f	G	a	C	b	E	d	G	f	C	a	E	b	G	d	C	f	E	a	G	b
C	d	E	g	G	b	C	d	E	f	G	a	C	b	E	d	G	f	C	a	E	b	G	d	C	f	E	a	G	b

This harmonica starts with hole 1 "C" (Do)

****

> There are 21, 23 and 26 hole "Japan/Korea" harmonicas.
> You lose low "G" on the 23 hole harmonica
> and you also lose hole 8 on the 21 hole harmonica.
> Most 23 and 24 hole harmonicas are available in all keys.

24 Hole Japan/Korea Harmonicas

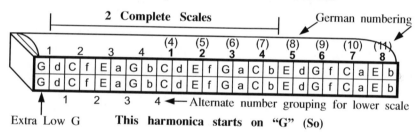

2 Complete Scales   German numbering

1		2		3		4 (4)		(5)		(6)		(7)		(8)		(9)		(10)		(11)	

| G | d | C | f | E | a | G | b | C | d | E | f | G | a | C | b | E | d | G | f | C | a | E | b |
| G | d | C | f | E | a | G | b | C | d | E | f | G | a | C | b | E | d | G | f | C | a | E | b |

Extra Low G   This harmonica starts on "G" (So)   ← Alternate number grouping for lower scale

Hohner's "Weekender" is the same configuration as the above harmonica.

****

> The Huang Musettes (tremolos) are a set of harmonicas in C and D flat.
> By stacking them, They can be played in any key (chromatically).

24 Hole Huang Harmonica

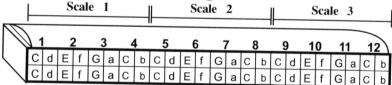

Scale 1   Scale 2   Scale 3

1		2		3		4		5		6		7		8		9		10		11		12	
C	d	E	f	G	a	C	b	C	d	E	f	G	a	C	b	C	d	E	f	G	a	C	b
C	d	E	f	G	a	C	b	C	d	E	f	G	a	C	b	C	d	E	f	G	a	C	b

This harmonica is based on the chromatic harmonica
Each scale is complete

41

Phil Duncan

Phil Duncan earned his Masters of Music Education degree in 1973 at the University of Missouri-Kansas City Conservatory of Music. His thesis focused on the study of methods for teaching the beginning student of any musical instrument. He has taught piano, guitar, and harmonica since the age of 16, having been introduced to the harmonica by his grandfather at age 7. With a versatile educator's experience ranging from elementary school through university levels, Phil served for 26 years in the Park Hill School District in Kansas City, Missouri. He taught vocal and general music in elementary, Junior High, Middle School and High School. During this tenure he did a five-year study on the use of the harmonica in the classroom. He is currently teaching at Park University in the Music Department. He instructs choir and voice as well as classes on Kansas City Jazz Style, American Folk Music and Music Education for Elementary Teachers.

As a clinician, Phil has conducted workshops at several harmonica conventions and at the University of Missouri-Kansas City, the University of Arkansas, the Texas Music Educator's Conference, and has presented many other clinics throughout the Midwest. He is also active in community education, and has advised teachers in techniques to better instruct their students in the art of playing the harmonica. He performs locally at Park University and many area community events and area churches. He is also active in the local harmonica club.

Phil's career as an author for Mel Bay Publications began in 1979 with the publication of The Deluxe Harmonica Method (93737BCD). This work was the result of ten years of research and two years of diligent writing. Since this auspicious beginning, Phil has published over 28 harmonica books with Mel Bay Publications on virtually every aspect of playing the harmonica, making a significant contribution to the repertoire for this instrument. He also has eight published instructional videos and is a recording artist with over 20 CD's to his credit. He has co-authored a book called *Power Harp* with the legendary Charlie Musselwhite.

He also performs on guitar and keyboard. Mel Bay has published his *Learn to Play Rock/Blues Electronic Keyboard* (94500VX). Missouri Middle Schools Journal published his article on teaching harmonica playing in the middle school. The Missouri Conservation Commission published several of his harmonica arrangements in its Songbook in 1982. He also is a contributor for the Society for the Preservation and Advancement's Harmonica Happenings news magazine.

Made in the USA
San Bernardino, CA
20 July 2015